POEMS OF REFLECTION AND RESILIENCE

Index

Dear Reader,

As you open the pages of "Poems of Reflection and Resilience," you embark on a journey not just through the chapters of a book, but through the layers of the human spirit. This collection is a personal exploration of the struggles and triumphs that shape us, the quiet moments of self-discovery, and the loud, defining events that redirect our paths.

Each poem in this book is a reflection of my own experiences with adversity and growth. They are born from moments of doubt, from the challenges of motherhood, and from the personal battles that have tested my strength and resolve. Yet, they are also born from moments of profound joy and realization, where resilience has proven to be not just necessary, but beautifully transformative.

This collection is divided into ten chapters, each focusing on a different aspect of the human experience. Through themes of awakening, battles, healing, and empowerment, I invite you to reflect on your own journey. Perhaps these words will resonate with your deepest struggles and inspire a recognition of your inner resilience.

I write these poems for you, the reader, as much as for myself. They are reminders that we are not alone in our experiences. My hope is that they offer comfort, provoke thought, and spark a conversation with your own inner self about what it means to grow and persevere.

Thank you for joining me on this path. May these poems bring you a sense of solidarity and strength as we navigate the complexities of life together.

With warmth and gratitude,

Elara

Awakening

The Quiet Strength

In the quiet,
beneath the clamor of the day,
I find the silent beats
of a heart unswayed.
Solitude whispers,
its voice soft but clear,
revealing the power
I hold near.
In stillness, a fortress,
in silence, a guide,
discovering strength
where true selves reside.

First Steps

Here at the start,
where the path shows its thorns,
I stand with my shadows,
my fears newly born.
Acknowledging each,
a whisper to the wind,
my journey begins
with the steps from within.
To see and to say,
to name each dark wave,
is the first stride taken
on the road to the brave.

Change's Embrace

Change comes like the dawn,
slow, then all at once,
coloring dark in hues of possibility.
Embracing its rhythm,
I dance to the song of transformation,
feet stepping forward in sync with growth.
With each turn, a landscape renewed,
a self reformed,
embracing change,
the truest path to bloom.

Battles

The Night's Watch

In the depth of night, my demons whisper,
Casting shadows, long and sinister.
Their voices, like ice, scrape against resolve,
In darkened hours, my fears evolve.
But with each breath, I draw my sword,
Crafted from will, each word a chord.
Striking at whispers that bind like chains,
In the heart of battle, my spirit remains.

Doubt's Labyrinth

Each morning unfolds a labyrinthine test,
Paths paved in the questions of a mind not
at rest.
With each step, the echoes of doubt
resound,
In this maze, my fears are profound.
Yet, with steadfast heart, I confront each
turn,
Learning to quench the fires that burn.
With each victory small, confidence grows,
Out of struggles, a stronger self flows.

Against the Current

Society's mold, a rigid frame,
Demands conformity, all the same.
Yet I stand firm, against the tide,
Resisting the pull where judgments reside.
In defiance, my true colors gleam,
Resplendent against the ordinary stream.
For in the battle to be one's own,
Lies the victory of a self fully known.

Healing

Whisper of the Woods

In the whisper of the woods, I find peace,
Leaves rustling tales of release.
The brook babbles of old pains washed
clear,
Under the canopy, I am removed from fear.
Nature's embrace heals every scar,
Each tree, a testament to how strong we
are.
Roots deeply set where no eyes see,
Reminding me to grow, to simply be.

Mending

Old wounds, like shadows, linger deep,
Haunting quiet moments as I sleep.
Yet, time weaves silver threads through grief,
Mending the fabric with gentle relief.
Step by slow step, the heart repairs,
With threads of memories, hopes, and cares.
Healing isn't hurried, nor swiftly done,
But through the pain, new strength is spun.

Grace of Self-Forgiveness

To err is human, to forgive, divine,
But the hardest grace is when the fault is
mine.
Forgiving oneself is a delicate art,
A dance of acceptance, a restart of the
heart.
In the mirror of my soul, I seek forgiveness'
face,
Learning to offer self the same embrace.
With each act of pardon, the spirit lightens,
And through self-forgiveness, the inner
world brightens.

Legacy

Maternal Echoes

Her voice, a soft echo in my daily deeds,
Guiding through storms, planting seeds.
In her eyes, a history untold,
In her arms, warmth in the cold.
Maternal whispers, threads through time,
In her wisdom, a rhythm, a rhyme.
Her love, the blueprint of my soul's design,
Forever a beacon, eternally mine.

Ancestral Threads

We are woven from threads, colors old and
bold,
Patterns of stories, our ancestors told.
In our veins, their dreams flow deep,
In our hearts, their hopes we keep.
Each gesture, each word, echoes a past,
Heritage that shapes us, shadows cast.
What we inherit is more than a name,
It's the resilience of those from whom we
came.

For Tomorrow's Child

What legacy to leave behind,
For the children of our kind?
Not just riches, nor mere words,
But love for life, for songs of birds.
Teach them kindness, show them care,
Nurture strength to do and dare.
May our legacy be a world renewed,
For every child, a future imbued.

Alone Together

Amid the Crowd

In the hum of crowded streets,
I walk unseen, my solace retreats.
Among the chatter, a silent scream,
In the multitude, an isolated dream.
The city breathes a lonely sigh,
Faces pass, unmet by eye.
Yet, in this sea where no one speaks,
My heart quietly, fervently seeks.

Tethers

In the whirl of life's relentless pace,
There are hands that halt, that embrace.
Connections that ground, that mend,
In the chaos, a family, a friend.
An anchor in the stormy tide,
Souls that stand by your side.
The bonds that hold, that save,
Tethers that anchor the brave.

Unexpected Haven

In the least of places, a gathering,
A shared smile, a song to sing.
In corners forgotten by the rushing day,
Community blooms in subtle array.
A nod, a laugh, a shared plight,
In these small joys, connection's light.
Where hearts converge in humble spaces,
We find our tribe in life's vast mazes.

Inner Voices

Dialogue Within

Alone with my thoughts, a dialogue begins,
Questions from corners where silence has
been.
"Who are you?" whispers my mind,
An echo responds, in kind.
Reflections surface, some dark, some
bright,
Conversations with myself, from morning to
night.
Each word, a step on the path to see,
The depths of the self, complex and free.

Whispers of Doubt

In the stillness, doubt whispers low,
A murmur from the shadows, an insidious
flow.
"Are you enough?" it taunts, unseen,
Chilling the air, where confidence had
been.
But in this quiet, I learn to reply,
To challenge each doubt, to refute every lie.
With every whisper, my resolve grows
strong,
In the silence, I find my belonging.

I Am

In the mirror of my mind, affirmations
glow,
"I am strong, I am worthy," they echo.
Against the tide of external measure,
These words are my treasure.
"I am enough," a mantra, a creed,
In these words, the power I need.
Self-worth affirmed with each recitation,
Building the foundation of my own
validation.

Growth

Echoes of the Past

From the echoes of the past, lessons are
drawn,
Like water from wells, from dusk till dawn.
Each memory a teacher, each scar a guide,
Showing paths once traveled, where pain
and wisdom reside.
Mistakes, the stonework of the fortress I
build,
With bricks of remorse, spaces filled.
Yet, from this structure, I learn to ascend,
Beyond the confines of what was, to what
will mend.

Forged in Fire

In the heat of struggle, my spirit was forged,
In the flames of adversity, my boundaries
gorged.
From the fire, not ash, but iron arose,
Molded by trials, through the blows.
Strength not given, but earned, and found,
In the deepest pits, on the hardest ground.
Adversity, the cruel yet wise artisan,
Crafting resilience with a master plan.

Shifting Views

Once, I saw myself through a glass, darkly,
Edges blurred, in shadows, starkly.
But time, the artist, paints anew,
In strokes of experience, changing the view.
With each layer added, perceptions shift,
From self-doubt to grace, a slow but sure
drift.
Now, in the mirror, a clearer sight,
Of who I am, in a truer light.

Reflections

Crossroads

At the crossroads of my yesterdays,
I pause to gaze down paths once paced.
Each choice, a stone in the mosaic of me,
Pivotal moments that set the journey free.
Reflecting on the crossroads, the turns I took,
The pages of my life, an open book.
In each decision, a story's fork,
In whispers of what was, I find my talk.

Mirrored Thoughts

In the mirror of time, I see shades of me,
Fragments of who I was, whispers of who
I'll be.
Mirrored thoughts of a past self, so near, yet
far,
A distant echo of the brightest star.
Who I used to be—haunting yet dear,
A specter of past, in the rearview clear.
Yet in this reflection, not just past I see,
But the seeds of future, sprouting free.

Embracing Reflections

Facing the mirror, a familiar sight,
A reflection worn, in the waning light.
Accepting the image, the lines, the grace,
Each scar, each smile, I embrace.
For in this reflection, I see true,
The beauty of age, of experiences through.
Acceptance, a gentle, yet powerful
correction,
Finding peace in my own reflection.

Horizon

Beyond the Horizon

Beyond the horizon, where dreams lie
awake,
In the quiet whisper of the morning about
to break.
Visions of what could be, floating free,
In that golden land, I see the future me.
Each dawn a canvas, new and bright,
Painted with hues of nascent light.
Dreams of tomorrow in my heart's hold,
A story of the future, yet to be told.

Unreached Summits

Goals like mountains, towering, steep,
Summits that call, their promises keep.
Each step a climb, a challenge, a test,
Towards peaks unseen, where ambitions
nest.
Not yet reached, these heights I spy,
But with each attempt, I'm drawn to try.
For in the pursuit, the journey's thrill,
Lies the strength gained, the iron will.

The Path Unfolds

The journey long, the path unknown,
Yet forward we move, the seeds now sown.
Roads wind and twist, under star and sun,
The voyage of life, never truly done.
With each mile traveled, a lesson learned,
In every departure, new dreams earned.
Though the end unseen, the map
uncharted,
With hopeful heart, the journey departed.

Empowerment

My Space

I claim this space, my rightful place,
In the world's vast, expansive embrace.
No longer small, nor quiet, nor tame,
I stand, I speak, I announce my name.
With every step, my path I pave,
In every breath, my banner wave.
This ground, my stage, this sky, my dome,
I claim each inch of this world as home.

The Power of No

No, a word, simple, yet profound,
A boundary set, a line around.
With each no spoken, strength I find,
In the spaces left behind.
No to demands that drain my spirit,
Yes to life and all near it.
In saying no, I take control,
Empower my body, feed my soul.

True Self

In the mirror, I now see,
The truest version staring back at me.
Not masked in guise, nor draped in
pretend,
But honest, unique, a genuine friend.
Embracing all, the flaws, the fire,
Each quirk and laugh, each unmet desire.
In authenticity, I am set free,
Celebrating the one and only me.